13 Architects
Children Should Know

Florian Heine

PRESTEL

Munich · London · New York

Contents

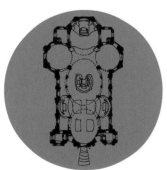

hether we go shopping, visit a church or museum, or simply take a walk in town, we are surrounded by architecture. Architecture is an art form that everyone can see and that in some way influences all of us. Good architecture helps make us feel comfortable in a house or pleased by a city.

We may not be fully aware of it, but architects are the people responsible for how everything looks around us. With their ideas, they have changed not only architectural styles but also building technologies. The way we make architecture has changed a lot in the last 200 years. Many buildings created nowadays would have been barely thinkable in times gone by. To help you learn more about how these changes took place, we will introduce you to 13 of the world's most famous architects.

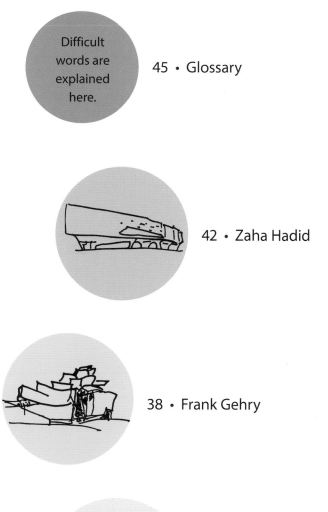

Gothic* period in Italy c. 1200–1400

Filippo Brunelleschi 1377–1446

1296 Construction started on the Basilica
of Santa Maria del Fiore, Florence

1379 The pope moves from exile in Avignon,
France back to the Vatican in Rome

1418–1428 San Lorenzo, Florence

1360   1365   1370   1375   1380   1385   1390   1395   1400   1405   1410   1415

Dome of the Basilica of Santa Maria del Fiore,
1420–1436, Florence

The fascinating thing about Brunelleschi's dome is that
there are actually two of them: the one inside that supports
all the weight and the outer one that protects the inner
one. This amazing construction took 16 years to build.

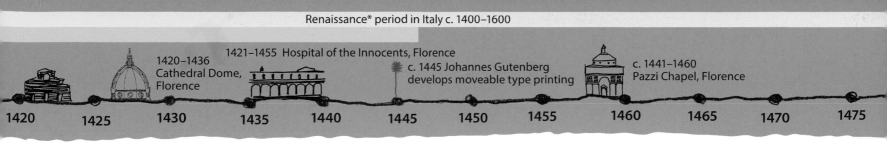
Renaissance* period in Italy c. 1400–1600

1420–1436
Cathedral Dome,
Florence

1421–1455 Hospital of the Innocents, Florence

c. 1445 Johannes Gutenberg
develops moveable type printing

c. 1441–1460
Pazzi Chapel, Florence

1420   1425   1430   1435   1440   1445   1450   1455   1460   1465   1470   1475

Filippo Brunelleschi

Brunelleschi was a goldsmith by trade, but he was much more interested in buildings—especially the buildings of antiquity*. Who would have thought that a broken egg would mark the beginning of his success story as an architect?

Born
 1377 in Florence
Died
 1446 in Florence,
 buried in the
 Cathedral of Florence
Education
 Goldsmith
Professions
 Sculptor, Architect,
 Inventor
Architectural Style
 Renaissance*

When building work started on the Basilica of Santa Maria del Fiore in Florence in 1296, everyone knew it would be among the biggest cathedrals in Christendom. Yet when the church was nearly finished, the builders realized they didn't have a clue how to construct its huge dome. The only dome of this size was on the Pantheon in Rome, and it was over 1,000 years old. Brunelleschi had studied this building in detail, and he knew how to build something like it in Florence.

But the city leaders did not trust Filippo at first, so they organized a competition in 1418. Whoever came up with the best idea for how to build such an enormous dome would get the commission. Brunelleschi knew the solution, but he was only willing to reveal it to the person who could rest an egg upright on top of a marble slab. Nobody in Florence managed to do this trick. Finally, Brunelleschi took the egg and pressed it down so hard against the slab that the shell flattened firmly and the egg stood still. The other master builders got very worked up, claiming they could have done the same thing. They probably could have, of course, but they simply didn't come up with the idea. As such, it was Filippo who went on to build the dome of the cathedral.

Good to know
Brunelleschi helped make another discovery that is still being used in art schools and by architects to this day: central perspective*. This is a way of drawing people, streets, and houses so that they look three-dimensional—even though we can only see them on flat paper.

5

Gothic* period in Italy c. 1200–1400

Filippo Brunelleschi 1377–1446

1418–1428 San Lorenzo, Florence

1420–1436 Cathedral Dome, Florence

1421–1455 Hospital of the Innocents, Florence

c. 1441–1460 Pazzi-Chapel, Florence

1360 1370 1380 1390 1400 1410 1420 1430 1440 1450 1460 1470

La Rotonda,
1566–1591, Vicenza

The Villa sits gracefully on its small hill. It has four temple facades, one for each side. The first time you see this building, you might not discover where the entrance exists.

Renaissance* period in Italy c. 1400–1600

Andrea Palladio 1508–1580

c. 1510 Copernicus determines that the Earth revolves around the Sun

1517 Martin Luther confronts the Catholic church with his Ninety-Five Theses

1577–1592 Il Redentore, Venice

1566–1591 La Rotonda, Vicenza

1480 1490 1500 1510 1520 1530 1540 1550 1560 1570 1580 1590

Andrea Palladio

Andrea di Piero della Gondola (Andrea Palladio) was the son of a stonemason—a highly trained construction worker. Palladio worked as a stonemason himself and as a sculptor before becoming an architect.

Born
1508 in Padua as Andrea di Piero della Gondola
Died
1580 in Vicenza
Education
Stonemason, Sculptor
Professions
Stonemason, Sculptor, Architect
Architectural Style
Renaissance*

Palladio may have been a stonemason his entire life had not one of his sponsors discovered his extraordinary talent. Conte Trissino taught Palladio everything about antiquity*. The Conte even traveled with him to Rome so he could study the ancient buildings. He also introduced him to important people who soon wanted the young architect to design their houses. Palladio developed a special way of designing buildings: he used elements of architecture from antiquity*. A very important aspect of this style was his so-called temple fronts or facades, which consisted of columns and triangular tops called pediments. The name "temple front" originates from ancient Greek and Roman temples (or religious buildings) that had similar columns and pediments to signify their special importance.

Palladio did not build temples, however, because people in his day did not worship ancient Greek and Roman gods. Instead, Andrea built mostly villas, which were large country houses for rich people. The families who commissioned these buildings loved Palladio's temple facades, because they gave their villas a much more elegant appearance. So what was once used in antiquity as a way of worshipping gods was now used by Palladio for making "normal" houses. This idea made Palladio's style all the rage in northern Italy. His most famous villa is

We do not know a great deal about Palladio's personal life. He is remembered mostly through his buildings, which still influence architects today. As it happens, Palladio never actually built a villa for himself. If you could design your very own villa, how would it look?

La Rotonda near Vicenza. It is so named because of its circular interior and the dome (or "Rotonda") above.

Palladio did not just build villas. He also designed a famous theatre in Vicenza and two big churches in Venice. Both of the churches have beautiful temple facades that can be seen from Venice's St. Mark's Square. Some of Palladio's greatest designs were never even built— including designs for Venice's famous Rialto Bridge and Doge's Palace.

Palladio's ideas became so popular, he wrote a book about them: "The Four Books of Architecture". Here he explained how to build not only these villas but also churches and even bridges. Architects all over the world would read his book and use its ideas. If you take a close look, you will recognize Palladio's style in all kinds of buildings. Even the home of the United States President, the White House, is a "Palladian" building.

Good to know
Andrea was given the name Palladio by Giangiorgio Trissino, who had sponsored him. The name is meant to remind us of Pallas Athena, the Greek goddess of wisdom and art.

**Il Redentore
(Church of the Most
Holy Redeemer),**
1577–1592, Venice

This church in Venice
was built as way of
saying thanks to God for
liberating the city from
the plague*. Even today,
people in Venice process
from the city center
in St. Mark's Square
to the church, which
lies over a canal. This
procession takes place
over a temporary "bridge"
made of boats, and it
has occurred every third
Sunday in July since 1577.

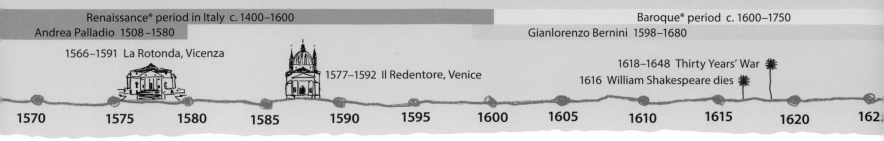

Renaissance* period in Italy c. 1400–1600
Andrea Palladio 1508–1580

Baroque* period c. 1600–1750
Gianlorenzo Bernini 1598–1680

1566–1591 La Rotonda, Vicenza

1577–1592 Il Redentore, Venice

1618–1648 Thirty Years' War
1616 William Shakespeare dies

1570   1575   1580   1585   1590   1595   1600   1605   1610   1615   1620   162.

Born
1598 in Naples
Died
1680 in Rome
Training
Sculptor
Professions
Sculptor, Architect,
Painter, Dramatist,
Caricaturist*
Building Style
Baroque*

Gianlorenzo Bernini

Gianlorenzo Bernini could do everything. He was the most famous sculptor of his day, and he could also paint, write plays, and make funny drawings called caricatures*. Bernini's buildings, too, are among the greatest of the 1600s.

With all of these special talents, Bernini attracted many important clients in Rome from an early age. His sculptures look quite different from those of the Renaissance* period, which often appear stiff and formal. Bernini's figures seem to come alive, and you can often recognize a sense of fear and determination in them.

Communicating feelings is a characteristic of art from the Baroque* period, the time when Bernini lived. And while Gianlorenzo was never actually trained as an architect, he still got commissions as a master builder. Like sculpting, architecture requires you to focus on form and shape and to arrange everything so that it all fits together. This is why many sculptors were also architects in earlier times. Michelangelo a sculptor, worked on many buildings in Rome before Bernini was born.

The first great work Bernini produced as an architect was the Baldachin*. It stands over the grave of St. Peter in St. Peter's Basilica, which is now in Vatican City. But Bernini did not do this work alone. He had the help of another great architect named Francesco Borromini. With its turned columns and curved roof, the Baldachin appears graceful and almost

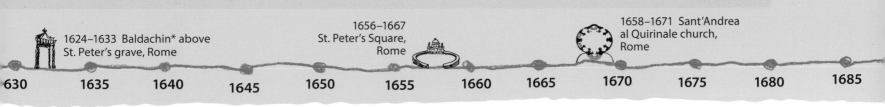

1624–1633 Baldachin* above
St. Peter's grave, Rome

1656–1667
St. Peter's Square,
Rome

1658–1671 Sant'Andrea
al Quirinale church,
Rome

630   1635   1640   1645   1650   1655   1660   1665   1670   1675   1680   1685

**Baldachin* above
the Grave of St. Peter,**
1624–1633, Rome

It's hard to tell that the
Baldachin is almost 98
feet (30 meters) high,
because St. Peter's
Basilica itself is so
massive. The church is,
after all, the biggest in
Christendom.

Quiz
Which famous architect
helped Bernini build
the Baldachin?
(Answer on page 46)

**St. Peter's Square
(Vatican Square),**
1656–1667, Rome

At 950 feet (290 meters)
long and 787 feet
(240 meters) wide, Vatican
Square is enormous.
The colonnades consist
of 284 pillars, each one
measuring 50 feet
(15 meters) in height.
On top of the pillars are
144 figures of holy saints,
each of them 10 feet
(3 meters) tall. As a
sculptor, Bernini created
many of them himself.

moving. It is actually 98 feet (30 meters) high, which is about the height of
an eight-story building.

Bernini created another important monument for St. Peter's: the huge plaza
(or forecourt) that stands in front of the church. Even here you can tell that
Bernini was a sculptor. The curved rows of columns on the square, which are
called colonnades, seem like enormous arms extending from the church.
In this way, Bernini was looking to show how the church welcomes all
people and brings them into its community.

In 1665, Bernini was summoned to Paris by King Louis XIV of France, because
he wanted him to build a new palace. His designs were not accepted by the
King, but they had a great influence on many other architects. One of these
artists was Christopher Wren (see page 14 /15), whom he got to know in Paris.

**Sant'Andrea al Quirinale,
(Church of St. Andrew
at the Quirinal),**
1658–1671, Rome

This tiny church has an oval ground plan*, which was totally new for the time. Even the staircase is circular and covered by a curved canopy.

**Sant'Andrea al Quirinale,
(Church of St. Andrew
at the Quirinal),**
Ground plan

The building's oval ground plan and curving shapes are typical of the Baroque* period.

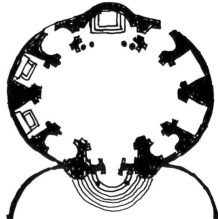

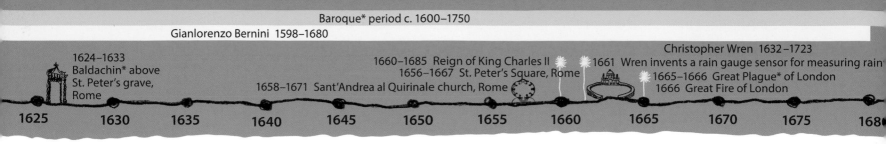
Baroque* period c. 1600–1750

Gianlorenzo Bernini 1598–1680

1624–1633
Baldachin* above
St. Peter's grave,
Rome

1660–1685 Reign of King Charles II
1656–1667 St. Peter's Square, Rome
1658–1671 Sant'Andrea al Quirinale church, Rome

Christopher Wren 1632–1723
1661 Wren invents a rain gauge sensor for measuring rain
1665–1666 Great Plague* of London
1666 Great Fire of London

1625　　1630　　1635　　1640　　1645　　1650　　1655　　1660　　1665　　1670　　1675　　168

Christopher Wren

Born
　1632 in East-Knoyle,
　England
Died
　1723 in Hampton
　Court, buried in
　St. Paul's Cathedral,
　London
Study
　Mathematics,
　Astronomy
Professions
　Professor of
　Astronomy, Architect
Architectural Style
　English Baroque*

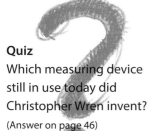

Quiz
Which measuring device
still in use today did
Christopher Wren invent?
(Answer on page 46)

Although Christopher Wren was a Professor of Astronomy in Oxford University, he decided he would much prefer to work as an architect.

Wren had already built a theatre in Oxford and a college in Cambridge when a fire broke out at a London bakery in September 1666. This fire spread throughout the city, leaving much of London in debris and ash. Over 13,000 houses and 87 churches were burnt to the ground, and many streets were destroyed.

Soon after the Great Fire, English King Charles II put a team together that would be responsible for reconstructing the city. One team member was Christopher Wren. Charles and Christopher knew each other well because they used to play together as children. And the king knew that Wren was not only good with mathematics and astronomy, but also with architecture.

Wren got right to work and designed plans for rebuilding the entire city. Up until his death in 1723, Wren built 52 churches that all varied in appearance. Today, 15 of these churches are still standing. Among them is the most beautiful and biggest of them all: St. Paul's Cathedral, one of London's most important landmarks.

Good to know
Christopher Wren's style looks a little like Renaissance* architecture. This is because he studied "The Four Books of Architecture" by Palladio, as well as drawings by many other famous architects, whom he wanted to imitate. And thankfully he achieved his goals. Wren's own cathedral—and above all its dome—would itself be imitated by later architects.

St. Paul's Cathedral,
1675–1709, London

With its mighty dome and two towers, St. Paul's was completed
in 1709. It took only about 35 years to build the church, which
was remarkably quick for such a giant building. Wren is one of
the few architects to witness the completion of a cathedral in
his lifetime. He was, however, almost 80 years old by that time.

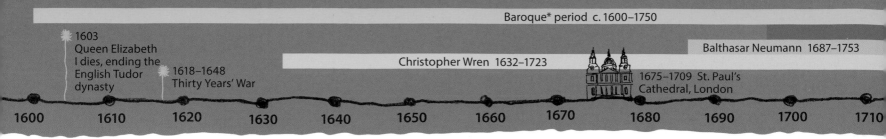

Baroque* period c. 1600–1750

1603
Queen Elizabeth I dies, ending the English Tudor dynasty

1618–1648
Thirty Years' War

Christopher Wren 1632–1723

Balthasar Neumann 1687–1753

1675–1709 St. Paul's Cathedral, London

1600 1610 1620 1630 1640 1650 1660 1670 1680 1690 1700 1710

Stairwell of the Würzburg Palace,
1719–1744, Würzburg

The vault of the ceiling is larger than two tennis courts, yet Neumann created it without using any supporting beams.

Quiz

Can you find the detail of Balthasar Neumann, as shown on page 17, in the picture here?

(Answer on page 46)

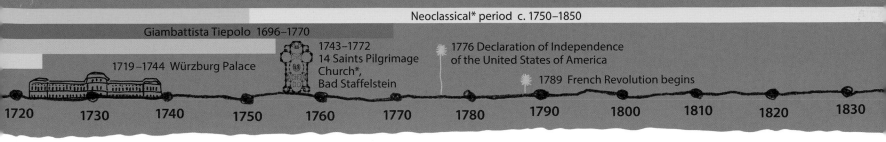

Neoclassical* period c. 1750–1850

Giambattista Tiepolo 1696–1770

1719–1744 Würzburg Palace

1743–1772
14 Saints Pilgrimage Church*,
Bad Staffelstein

1776 Declaration of Independence of the United States of America

1789 French Revolution begins

1720 1730 1740 1750 1760 1770 1780 1790 1800 1810 1820 1830

Balthasar Neumann

Nobody would have guessed that a simple bell and gun maker could become one of the greatest architects of his time.

Following school, Balthasar Neumann trained to be a bell and gun maker. Above all he learned how to make weapons. But that was not enough for him, so he studied to become a "pyrotechnics" specialist as well. Neumann became very familiar with explosives and knew how to put on a beautiful fireworks display. And just for good measure, he was trained as a civil and military engineer. All of these studies helped him become an important architect.

When the Prince-Bishop of Würzburg, Johann Philipp Franz von Schönborn, wanted a new palace, he made Neumann the director of the huge building project in 1720. This was a daring choice, because

Born
 1687 in Eger, in today's Czech Republic
Died
 1753 in Würzburg
Education and Professions
 Bell & Gun Maker, Fireworks Specialist, Architect
Architectural Style
 Late Baroque*

Stairwell of the Würzburg Palace, Detail

Because Tiepolo and Neumann had a very good understanding, the painter immortalized Balthasar in the ceiling fresco*. You can see the architect, who had managed to become a colonel in the military, leaning quite casually against a canon. And he's almost in the center of the painting—a great honor indeed!

Neumann was very young and had little experience at that time. The
Prince-Bishop gave Neumann his full trust, and he was not disappointed.
When the architect died in 1753, he had created the most sophisticated
and extraordinary of all Baroque palaces. Today, the Würzburg Palace is
a UNESCO World Heritage Site*.

The main feature of this palace is the stairwell. Nowadays it might be a bit
strange to say that. But in the Baroque era, the stairwell was something
very important. It was there where the Prince-Bishop received his guests.
And while these guests climbed the stairs, they were able to see more and
more of this amazing room built by Neumann. The famous Italian painter
Giambattista Tiepolo was sent from Naples to decorate the ceiling, which
included the largest continuous fresco* in the world.

Pilgrimage Church*
of the 14 Saints,
Right: Ground plan
Above: Façade

Like Bernini did in his
Sant'Andrea al Quirinale
(Church of St. Andrew at
the Quirinal), Balthasar
Neumann also used an
oval shape for his ground
plan. However, he didn't
stop at one oval! He
interwove several oval
shapes into each other.

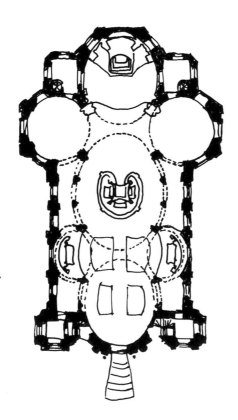

Neumann did not just work on the
Würzburg Palace. In fact, it is said that
he built "more than a hundred famous
bridges, churches, abbeys, castles, and
houses." The most impressive of his
churches may be the Pilgrimage Church*
of the 14 Saints in the German region
of Franconia, which he started in 1743.
Unfortunately, this building was not
finished until after his death.

Pilgrimage Church*
of the 14 Saints,
1743–1772,
Bad Staffelstein

Because Neumann used
the oval shape as the
basic form of his ground
plan, the walls and vaults
appear to sway. This was
called curved architecture
and was typical of the
late Baroque* period.
Neumann could design
in this style like hardly
anyone else.

Baroque* period c. 1600–1750

Thomas Jefferson 1743–1826

Balthasar Neumann 1687–1753

1776 Declaration of Independence of the United States of America

1743–1772 14 Saints Pilgrimage Church*, Bad Staffelstein

1719–1744 Würzburg Palace

1768–1809 Monticello, Charlottesville

1720 1725 1730 1735 1740 1745 1750 1755 1760 1765 1770 1775

Thomas Jefferson

Sometimes you wonder how certain people can organize all their talents and still have time for everything. Thomas Jefferson was just such a person.

Born
1743 in Shadwell near Charlottesville, Virginia

Died
1826 in Monticello near Charlottesville, Virginia

Study
Law

Professions
Lawyer, Architect, Governor of Virginia, Diplomat, President of the United States

Architectural Style
Neoclassical*

Quiz
Jefferson did not design the University of Virginia on his own. The English-American architect Benjamin Latrobe (1764–1820) helped him with it. Latrobe came to America in 1796 and became the United States' first professional architect. Do you know what building is his most famous?

(Answer on page 46)

Thomas Jefferson taught himself everything he knew about architecture. Much of what he knew came from his many trips to Europe, and what he had not seen in person he simply read about in books. When designing his own country estate "Monticello" near Charlottesville, Virginia from 1770, he used ideas from Palladio's "Four Books of Architecture". If you look closely at Monticello, you'll see how similar it is to the villas of Palladio (see pages 6-9), with its columns, pediment, and dome.

In the 1780s, Jefferson was asked to design the state capitol building of Virginia in Richmond. Here he used a Neoclassical* architectural style. Jefferson also designed an entire university—the University of Virginia in Charlottesville. This was the first American campus university. Its buildings were grouped around a big lawn area, much like you see in many universities nowadays. At the center of the campus was the library, a big domed building designed to look like the Pantheon in Rome. Americans greatly admired Jefferson's architecture, perhaps because it reminded them of the powerful Roman Republic. Jefferson, of course, became America's third President, and he helped create a republican* form of government for the young United States.

Many American architects who followed Thomas Jefferson built state capitols and other public buildings in his Neoclassical style.

Good to know
Monticello and Thomas Jefferson are portrayed on the American nickel, or 5 cent coin.

20

Neoclassical* period c. 1750–1850

1785–1788 Virginia
State Capitol, Richmond

1789 French Revolution begins

1793–1823 United States
Capitol building, built
by Benjamin Latrobe

1817–1826 University
of Virginia, Charlottesville

780   1785   1790   1795   1800   1805   1810   1815   1820   1825   1830   1835

Facade of Monticello,
Sketch

This early sketch of
Monticello was made
by Jefferson himself.

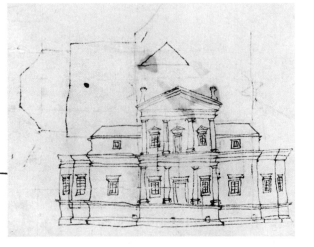

Monticello, 1768–1809,
Charlottesville, Virginia

Jefferson was happiest
at his country home,
"Monticello", which he
constantly rebuilt and
extended up to his death.
Today it is a museum,
where you can see the
inventions and collections
of one of America's most
famous leaders.

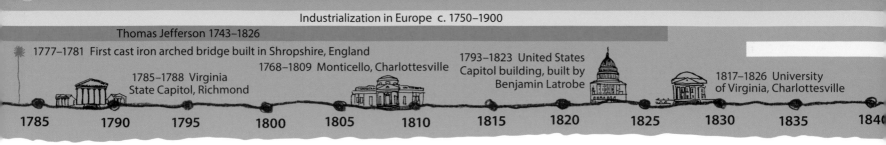

Industrialization in Europe c. 1750–1900

Thomas Jefferson 1743–1826

1777–1781 First cast iron arched bridge built in Shropshire, England

1768–1809 Monticello, Charlottesville

1785–1788 Virginia State Capitol, Richmond

1793–1823 United States Capitol building, built by Benjamin Latrobe

1817–1826 University of Virginia, Charlottesville

1785 1790 1795 1800 1805 1810 1815 1820 1825 1830 1835 1840

Born
1832 in Dijon, as Gustave Bönick-hausen. He took the name Eiffel as a reminder of the Eifel, the homeland region of his ancestors.
Died
1923 in Paris
Study
Chemistry
Professions
Explosives Manufacturer, Civil Engineer, Architect
Architectural Style
Functionalism

Gustave Eiffel

Eiffel did not build palaces or churches. Instead, he designed railway bridges and other practical buildings out of steel. But his most famous design was a giant tower that came to symbolize the city of Paris.

Gustave Eiffel was not trained as an architect. He was an engineer by profession. Architects are primarily responsible for how a building looks, while engineers figure out how to turn the architect's ideas into a real structure—one that does not come crashing down! But Eiffel often had to be both an architect and an engineer at the same time. And he was proud of his designs. As he said: "Are we to understand that there is no beauty in our designs just because we are engineers?"

Until he set up his own business, Eiffel worked for a railway company and was responsible for building bridges all over the world. Yet his most well-known building project was done much closer to home. The Eiffel Tower in Paris, which was named after him, became part of the World's Fair of 1889. Gustave built the tower quicky and solidly, using the same material he had employed in his bridges—steel. Most of the tower's 18,000 construction pieces were pre-fabricated* in his own factory. They were then shipped across the river Seine and put together using over 2.5 million rivets. The whole project took less than 2 years to complete.

Many people did not like the tower at first. They called it the "skinny pyramid of iron ladders". In fact, the building was supposed to be taken down after 20 years. But Eiffel's tower gradually became admired. After all, at over 985 feet (300 meters) in height, it was the tallest structure in the world for many years! Today it is Paris's main tourist attraction.

Art Nouveau period c. 1895–1910

1832–1923 Gustave Eiffel

1853 Elisha Otis helps create the modern elevator

1876–1877 Ponte della Maria Pia bridge, Porto

1879–1886 Statue of Liberty erected in New York

1887–1889 Eiffel Tower, Paris
1889 World's Fair, Paris

1845 1850 1855 1860 1865 1870 1875 1880 1885 1890 1895 1900

Eiffel Tower,
1887–1889, Paris

To stop the Eiffel Tower from becoming rusted, it has to be freshly painted every 7 years. Each re-painting takes about 18 months to complete. The tower's color has changed over the years. It was painted red at first, and was once even yellow.

Steel Supports of the Statue of Liberty,
1879–1886, New York

Eiffel was also involved in the construction of the Statue of Liberty. As an engineer, Eiffel designed the interior support beams of this almost 330 feet (100 meters) tall structure, as well as the two spiral staircases that you can use to climb up to its head.

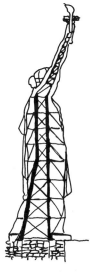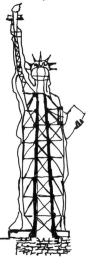

c. 1895–1910 Art Nouveau period

From 1883
La Sagrada Família,
Barcelona

1879–1886 Statue
of Liberty erected
in New York

1887–1889 Eiffel Tower, Paris
1887 Arthur Conan Doyle publishes
the first Sherlock Holmes story

1900–1914 Park Güell, Barcelona

1880   1882   1884   1886   1888   1890   1892   1894   1896   1898   1900   190

La Sagrada Família,
from 1883, Barcelona

The cathedral of La
Sagrada Família, which
was financed by dona-
tions, is still not fully
completed. It should
be finished on the 100th
anniversary of Gaudí's
death in 2026. That
means the whole con-
struction will have taken
over 144 years, longer
than it took to build
St. Peter's Basilica in
Rome.

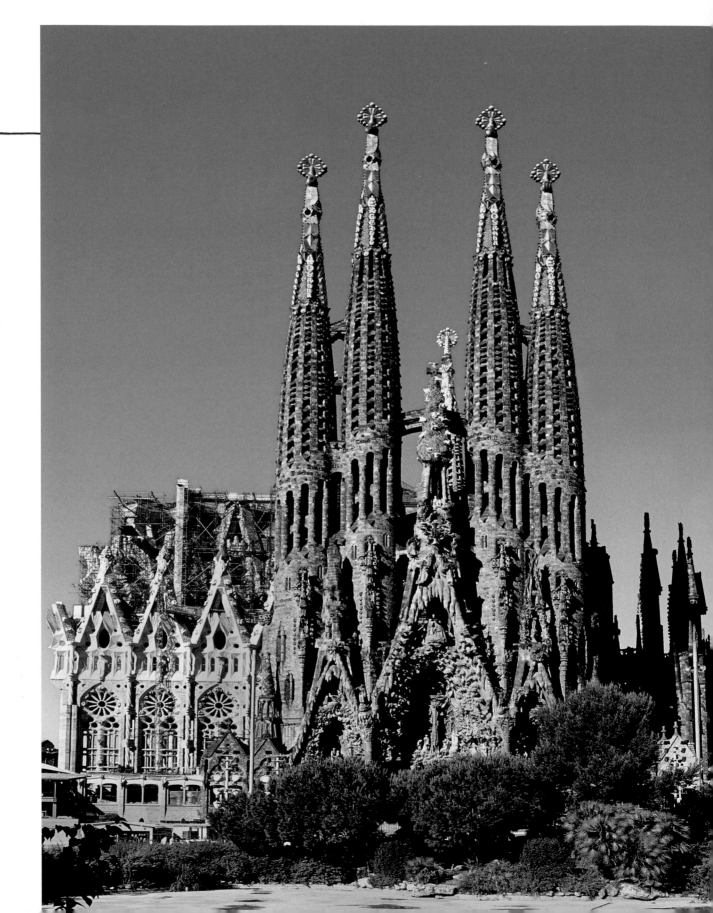

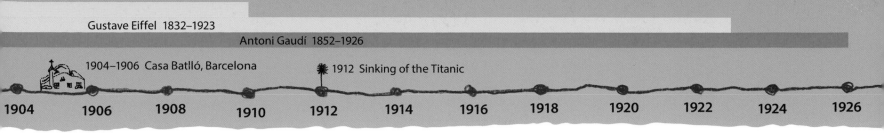

Antoni Gaudí

"Who knows if we have given the title to a lunatic or a genius—only time will tell us."

Born
  1852 in Reus,
  Catalonia
Died
  1926 in Barcelona
Study and Profession
  Architect
Architectural Style
  Art Nouveau

This is what the director of Barcelona's School of Architecture said in 1878 at Antoni Gaudí's graduation. Gaudí had barely gotten through the university, but he was regarded as an extremely good illustrator. And he was lucky, too! That same year he came to know the business leader Eusebi Güell, who encouraged the young architect and became an important patron.

During his studies, Gaudí was very interested in Gothic* architecture and the building style of the Moors* in Spain. Added to that, he had always carefully observed and drawn nature from his childhood. Antoni mixed these interests together into a special, personal style. Many of Gaudí's buildings do not look as if they had been planned, but had grown out of the earth. They seem to resemble living beings. For example, his Casa Batlló from 1906 has a roof that looks like a dragon's back.

Gaudí's best-known structure is the cathedral called La Sagrada Família, which he began designing at age 31. Even here, his architectural style appears like that of a living organism—constantly growing and growing. The pillars and vaults have the feel of trees and branches and the facades are like giant sandcastles. Yet the construction of this church is very complicated and precise.

Park Güell, 1900–1914,
Barcelona

Eusebi Güell wanted to
build a park in the north
of Barcelona. Gaudí
designed it between
1910 and 1914. It is as
popular today as it was
back then.

Although Gaudí became a successful and sought-after architect, by 1918
he had abandoned all other building projects except the cathedral. He
could not be bothered with anything else, even the way he dressed. On
June 7th 1926, he was run over by a streetcar right in front of the Sagrada
Família. And because he looked so scruffy, nobody recognized him. So
he was taken to a hospital for the poor and not treated properly. He died
of his wounds after three days, but was later buried in the crypt of the
Sagrada Família.

Today, Gaudí's buildings are the most important and well-known in
Barcelona. So it seems he was much more of a genius than a mad-man!

Casa Batlló, 1904–1906, Barcelona

With this building, Gaudí tells the story of St. George. He is the patron saint of Catalonia, the home region of Barcelona in Spain. St. George saved a village from a dragon … and the roof of Casa Batlló looks like the scales of that dragon.

Modernism* c. 1918–1970

Antoni Gaudí 1852–1926

Frank Lloyd Wright 1867–1959

1900–1914 Park Güell, Barcelona

From 1883
La Sagrada Família,
Barcelona

1904–1906 Casa Batlló, Barcelona

1914–1918 First World War

1892 1895 1898 1901 1904 1907 1910 1913 1916 1919 1922 1925

Fallingwater, 1935–1937, Pennsylvania

Fallingwater was used from 1937 to 1963 as a holiday
home by the Kaufmann family, who hired Wright to
design the house. It is now a much visited museum.

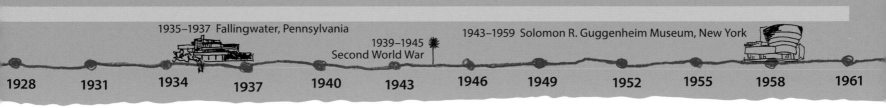
Frank Lloyd Wright

Frank Lloyd Wright was the first architect to talk about "organic architecture". His buildings needed to fit into their surroundings—into nature—and to suit the people who lived and worked in them.

Born
  1867 in Richland Center, Wisconsin
Died
  1959 in Phoenix, Arizona
Study
  Building Engineering
Profession
  Architect
Architectural Style
  Modernism*, Organic Architecture

Two of Wright's best known buildings are so different, it's hard to believe they were designed by the same architect. And this difference has little to do with the fact that one is a family home and the other is a museum.

Wright started his career in Chicago, Illinois. By about 1900, he created a style of house that looked flat and low to the ground. Wright did this because he wanted his homes to blend in with their surroundings—the flat landscape of Illinois. These houses typically had roofs, balconies, and windows that seemed to wrap themselves around the walls. Wright also designed the houses' insides in a new way. Most homes at that time had small rooms for every activity: sleeping, eating, reading, etc. In Wright's homes, different rooms often had no walls separating them—making them seem to flow into one other. Wright called his new kind of house the "Prairie house", after the flat prairie grasslands of America's Midwest.

In the 1930s, Wright began to build homes that were even roomier on the inside and more in tune with their environment. The most well-known of these, called "Fallingwater", is built directly above a waterfall. Wright chose this spot because it was the place where his client most liked to sit on his property. Fallingwater seems almost a part of the waterfall. The concrete slabs look like real rocks, and through the big windows you get the feeling of sitting directly in the countryside.

Good to know
Frank Lloyd Wright was one of the most important American architects of the last century. Over his sixty year career, he worked on more than 500 projects.

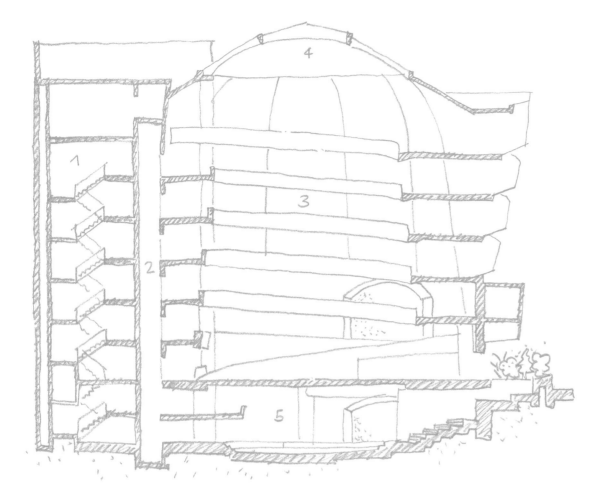

1   STAIRWELL

2   ELEVATOR

3   EXHIBITION

4   DOME LIGHT

5   AUDITORIUM

Good to know
Besides his building projects, Wright also ran a private school for architecture. Wright used to meet up with his students at his home on Sundays. There they would cook together, talk architecture, play music, and sing.

How different then does his Guggenheim Museum in New York look! The building crawls upwards like a giant caterpillar. Wright was not particularly fond of New York. There were too many people for his liking and it was too densely built up. So he designed a building that did not blend into its environment at all. It was made to stand out from the boxy skyscrapers that Wright disliked.

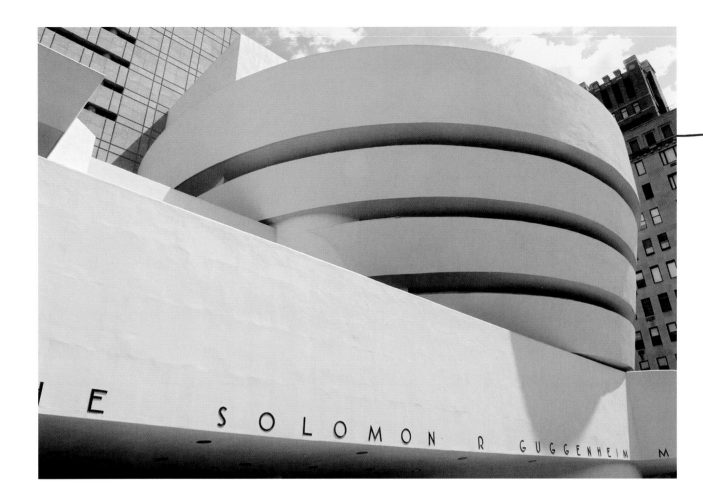

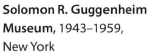

Solomon R. Guggenheim Museum, 1943–1959, New York

Wright began planning the Guggenheim Museum in 1943. But it was not officially opened until 1959, half a year after Wright's death. Many critics disliked the building because it seemed to be stealing the limelight from the art on display.

Solomon R. Guggenheim Museum, Interior View

Museums can often feel so cramped that you decide to miss a whole room of exhibits. This is simply not possible with New York's Guggenheim. You take an elevator right to the top and then wind your way down to the bottom. As you walk downward, you see every piece on show. We think that is very practical!

Modernism* c. 1918–1970

Frank Lloyd Wright 1867–1959

Ludwig Mies van der Rohe 1886–1969

1911 Roald Amundsen becomes the first man to reach the South Pole

1914–1918 First World War

1926 Foundation of the Bauhaus* art school in Dessau

1929 German Pavilion, Barcelona

1901 1904 1907 1910 1913 1916 1919 1922 1925 1928 1931 193

German Pavilion, 1929, Barcelona

In 1929, only three years after the death of Antoni Gaudí, Mies set up his famous exhibition pavilion in Barcelona.

A conversation between the two architects Gaudí and Mies van der Rohe would have been interesting if you think about how different their buildings are. Try to draw a building that the two of them might have planned together.

1935–1937 Fallingwater, Pennsylvania
1938 Mies immigrates to America
1939–1945 Second World War

1955–1959 Seagram Building, New York

1943–1959 Solomon R. Guggenheim Museum, New York

1937   1940   1943   1946   1949   1952   1955   1958   1961   1964   1967   1970

Ludwig Mies van der Rohe

Mies was already a great architect before he left Germany to escape the National Socialists (the Nazis) in 1938. He moved to America and eventually settled in Chicago.

For most of his career, Mies was both an architect and a teacher. While still in Germany, he served as head of the Bauhaus* in Dessau—an important school for art and architecture. He also designed the famous German pavilion for the 1929 World's Fair in Barcelona, Spain. This "house" was never meant to be lived in. Mies wanted to show how an architect might prefer to build if he concentrated on architecture alone, and not on the wishes of clients. So Mies designed a flat structure whose roof was supported by steel support beams and not by walls. He also used precious materials such as marble and onyx. Mies was not interested in decorating his buildings with anything fancy or ornamental. But what he did build had to be perfectly formed. This was the special thing about his building style. As he summed it up in his famous sentence: "Less is more."

Born
   1886 in Aachen as Maria Ludwig Michael Mies. Rohe is his mother's maiden name.
Died
   1969 in Chicago
Training
   Bricklayer, Visual Artist
Professions
   Draftsman, Architect, Professor of Architecture, Director of Bauhaus* in Dessau
Architectural Style
   Modernism*

Architecture can sometimes be praised for what the designer leaves out. In his famous Seagram Building, which was built in New York between 1955 and 1959, Mies used only half of the construction site available to him. Because land was so expensive in New York, architects typically made full

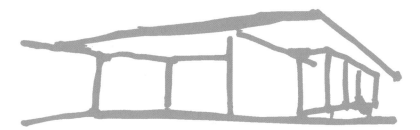

German Pavilion,
Interior View

It's hard to imagine how a family could live here. Where would they put the children's room, toys, bookshelves, and fluffy sofa? The only pieces of furniture standing there were designed by Mies himself. They were created for the Spanish royal couple, should they want to view the pavilion during their tour of the exhibition.

use of their building space and erected the skyscrapers close to the street. And to avoid making the streets too dark below, it was necessary to build structures that became narrower the higher up they got. Mies, on the other hand, wanted to build his skyscraper using a simple, strong, rectangular shape—just as wide at the top as it was at the bottom. So he convinced his clients to use only half of the building plot and to set aside a big square in front of the tall tower. This unusual idea not only kept his rectangular skyscraper from darkening the street below, it also gave New Yorkers and tourists alike a happy "plaza" where they could relax.

Seagram Building,
1955–1959, New York

When you first look at it, Mies' skyscraper does not seem to be anything out of the ordinary. Yet he achieved something here that few architects could —he made a building that was perfectly and precisely formed, down to the finest detail. In this way Mies had a huge influence on architects who came after him.

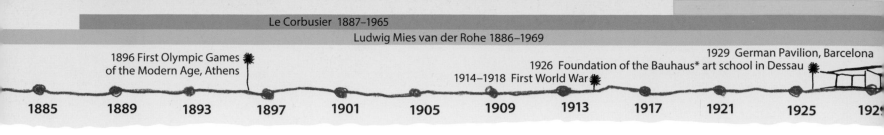

Le Corbusier 1887–1965
Ludwig Mies van der Rohe 1886–1969

1896 First Olympic Games
of the Modern Age, Athens

1929 German Pavilion, Barcelona
1926 Foundation of the Bauhaus* art school in Dessau
1914–1918 First World War

1885 1889 1893 1897 1901 1905 1909 1913 1917 1921 1925 1929

Born
  1887 in La Chaux-de-
  Fonds, Switzerland,
  as Charles-Édouard
  Jeanneret
Died
  1965 in Cap-Martin
  near Nice, France
Training
  Engraver
Study and Profession
  Architect
Architectural Style
  Modernism*

Le Corbusier

Charles-Edouard Jeanneret was a universal talent. He was a painter, artist, urban planner, and most of all an architect. From 1920, he called himself Le Corbusier.

The first house Le Corbusier built was in 1905, when he was only 18 years old. He trained with the most modern architects of his time in Paris, Vienna, and Berlin, before he finally set up his own architecture studio in Paris with his cousin, Pierre Jeanneret. Le Corbusier was interested in everything that had to do with modern art and modern technology, which is why he named his studio "The Laboratory for Modern Architecture".

Corbusier also built huge high-rises which he called "Living Machines". In these living machines, there were not just apartments but also shops,

**Architectural Model
for the "Plan Voisin"
(Neighborhood Plan)
of central Paris**
1922–1925

In 1925, Le Corbusier designed a plan for Paris. He wanted to demolish the old part of the city and have most Parisians live in 18 sixty-story high-rises. Luckily, this plan did not work out!

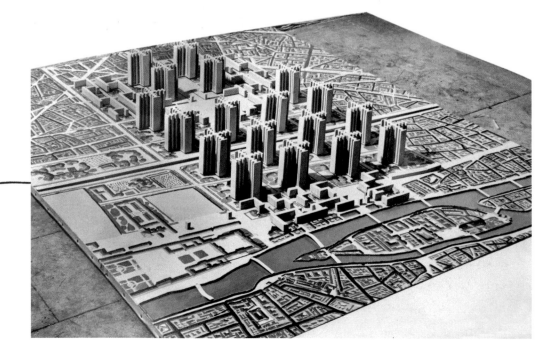

36

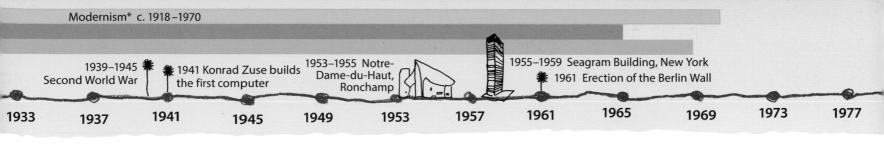

Modernism* c. 1918–1970

1939–1945
Second World War

1941 Konrad Zuse builds
the first computer

1953–1955 Notre-
Dame-du-Haut,
Ronchamp

1955–1959 Seagram Building, New York
1961 Erection of the Berlin Wall

1933   1937   1941   1945   1949   1953   1957   1961   1965   1969   1973   1977

**Notre-Dame-du-Haut,
Pilgrim's Church,**
1953–1955, Ronchamp

In contrast to the cold
high-rises of Le Corbusier,
this little church has a
tender and inviting feel
about it—even though
it's mostly made in con-
crete.

theatres, hotels, rooftop playgrounds, and everything a small town required
in just one building.

In 1955, Le Corbusier built the small Notre-Dame-du-Haut pilgrimage
church* near Ronchamp in France. On visiting this church as a pilgrim, you
get the feeling that it is growing out of the hill. The dark roof seems to hov-
er over the walls, because Le Corbusier actually placed it on small stilts that
you can hardly see. It is a very small church, so when too many pilgrims turn
up on certain days, masses have to be said outside. Fortunately, Le Corbusier designed the building's east wall as an open nave.*

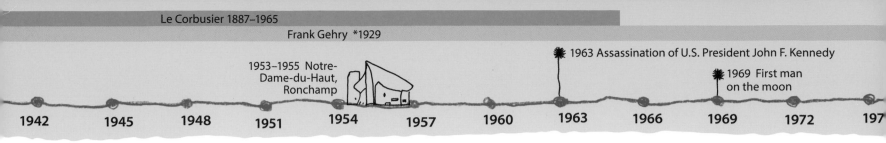

Le Corbusier 1887–1965

Frank Gehry *1929

1953–1955 Notre-
Dame-du-Haut,
Ronchamp

1963 Assassination of U.S. President John F. Kennedy

1969 First man
on the moon

1942　　1945　　1948　　1951　　1954　　1957　　1960　　1963　　1966　　1969　　1972　　197

Born
　1929 in Toronto,
　Canada, as Ephraim
　Owen Goldberg
Study
　Architecture,
　Urban Planning
Professions
　Truck Driver, Architect
Architectural Style
　Deconstructivism*

Frank Gehry

Frank Gehry achieved something that no architect before him had managed to do: he made a guest appearance on The Simpsons to show how he designed his buildings!

As a youngster, Frank always used to make models from pieces of wood with his grandmother. He built streets, houses, and whole towns. Later on, when it came to the question of what he wanted to do in life, he recalled the model-making sessions with his granny and thought: "That is what I want as a profession." And sometimes, his buildings really look as if a kid had been playing around with enormous blocks of wood.

Gehry was already a respected architect in 1993, when he received the commission to construct a new museum in the Spanish port city of Bilbao. The goal was to make this museum something very special, and that is what he achieved. Gehry built one of the most spectacular museums in the world. Never before had a museum looked like this one: it had the feel of a giant sculpture. It's look is even more astounding when you see Gehry's first sketches. You can only guess at what the final building is going to be. Gehry managed to create a museum that changed the whole city and the way people viewed it.

Guggenheim Museum,
Sketch

Gehry used a special computer program to design the building. This helped him convert his sketches into something that could actually be built.

38

1997 First volume of Harry Potter books appears

1996–2003 Walt Disney Concert Hall, Los Angeles

1993–1997 Guggenheim
Museum, Bilbao

2007 First i-Phone
goes on sale

1978   1981   1984   1987   1990   1993   1996   1999   2002   2005   2008   2011

Guggenheim Museum,
1993–1997, Bilbao

Since the opening of the Guggenheim Museum in 1997, more people visit the city than actually live there.

Further reading
Visit www.guggenheim-bilbao.es to see the museum in Bilbao and its art collection. You can also learn how the museum was built.

**Walt Disney Concert
Hall,** 1996–2003,
Los Angeles

Gehry built the Walt
Disney Concert Hall in
Los Angeles, where you
can clearly see his personal style on the project.
Maybe one day, Gehry
will make an appearance
in a Disney movie …

Gehry became globally famous
through his extraordinary
structures. These building not
only use unusual shapes, but
also unusual materials. Frank
sometimes built with titanium,
which was typically used for
aircraft construction. The colors
of the Bilbao Guggenheim
change because of its titanium
covering, always depending
on how the light falls upon
it. In this way, Gehry was able
to create a building style that
was immediately recognizable.
After the Guggenheim was
completed, many cities wanted
to have a Gehry building so
that they could attract as many
tourists as Bilbao.

Good to know
An English journalist
wrote that the museum
looked like a spaceship
that had landed 100
years ago. It doesn't
resemble the surrounding
buildings, but it fits into its
environment so well you
might think it had been
standing there for years.

**Before Frank Gehry had even
built a house, he used to make
many models using different
types of materials such as card-
board or tin. Try it yourself!**

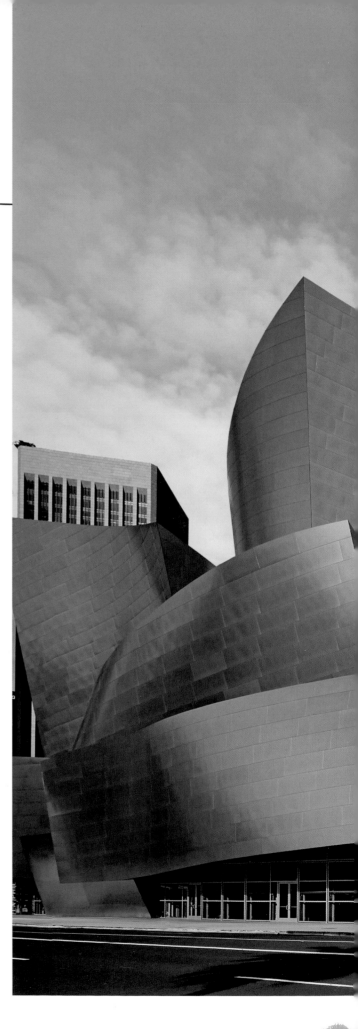

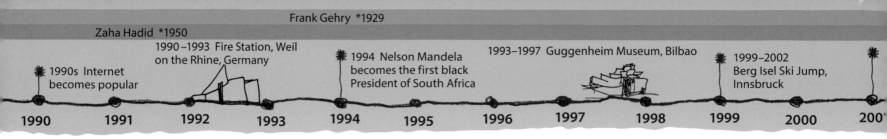

Frank Gehry *1929

Zaha Hadid *1950

1990–1993 Fire Station, Weil on the Rhine, Germany

1994 Nelson Mandela becomes the first black President of South Africa

1993–1997 Guggenheim Museum, Bilbao

1999–2002 Berg Isel Ski Jump, Innsbruck

1990s Internet becomes popular

1990 1991 1992 1993 1994 1995 1996 1997 1998 1999 2000 2001

Born
  1950 in Baghdad, Iraq, is now a British national
Study
  Mathematics, Architecture
Profession
  Architect
Architectural Style
  Deconstructivism*

Zaha Hadid

Zaha Hadid is the best-known female architect in the world. In 2004, she won the Pritzker Prize, the so-called "Nobel Prize for Architecture".

It may sound strange, but you can become well-known as an architect even if you build nothing at all. That is what happened to Zaha Hadid. Even though she had had her own architectural studio since 1980, she did not actually construct her first building until 1993. It was a fire station in the town of Weil on the Rhine, Germany. Up till then, Hadid had won many competitions, and her ideas, designs, and drawings became very well-known. Yet developers didn't really believe that such things could be built. Her ideas seemed too modern and ground-breaking.

During this time, Hadid taught at universities in America and Europe and also worked as a designer, which she still does today. After proving she could actually build one of her designs, she received more and more projects. Her office nowadays employs over 300 people, working on dozens of projects worldwide.

Phaeno Science Center, Sketch

As with Frank Gehry's sketches, Zaha Hadid's first drafts of a building seem very confusing. But the outcome is something extraordinary!

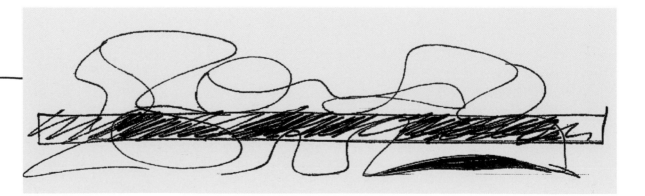

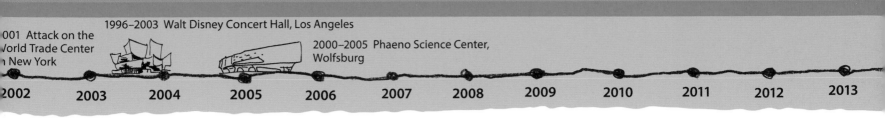

001 Attack on the
World Trade Center
in New York

1996–2003 Walt Disney Concert Hall, Los Angeles

2000–2005 Phaeno Science Center,
Wolfsburg

2002   2003   2004   2005   2006   2007   2008   2009   2010   2011   2012   2013

"My buildings should flow and bring energy to their surroundings", said Hadid. She achieves this goal time and time again, in all kinds of buildings. These include a science museum called the Phaeno Science Center, which opened in Wolfsburg, Germany in 2005; and the MAXXI art museum in Rome, completed in 2010. They also include tiny buildings such as tram stops and ski jumps.

Phaeno Science Center,
2000–2005, Wolfsburg

At first sight, the Phaeno looks like a huge lump of concrete. But in reality it seems to float on its 10 concrete support cones.

Good to know
In 1983, Zaha Hadid won her first major prize for architecture for "Le Peak", a leisure club in Hong Kong. Unfortunately, she did not build the club. Yet she was very proud that no single right angle could be found in her design.

Berg Isel Ski Jump,
1999–2002, Innsbruck

Hadid's dynamic style seems perfect for a Ski Jump. She designed this one like a huge snake that winds up to the top. Up above the jump is a café from where you can watch the ski jumpers.

Good to know
In 2002, Hadid's Ski Jump won for her the Austrian State Prize for Architecture.

Quiz
For which pop-music group did Zaha Hadid design a Tour Stage?
(Answer on page 46)

Hadid's career shows that women can become world-famous architects – something that was hardly possible in the past. As Zaha always says to her students, both male and female: "Believe in yourself—and you will become someone!"

Leabharlanna Poibli Chathair Baile Átha Cliath
Dublin City Public Libraries

Glossary

ANTIQUITY Antiquity is the era of the ancient Greeks and Romans from about 1,000BC to 500AD. Greek and Roman culture was almost entirely forgotten in the Middle Ages and was rediscovered in the Renaissance period.

BALDACHIN A baldachin is a canopy (or covering) of an altar or other holy site in a church. Some baldachins resemble fancy buildings.

BAROQUE Baroque is the term used for the chief architectural style between 1600 and 1750. In Baroque buildings, there are often curved facades and walls, as well as complicated layouts. Baroque architecture can be theatrical and very ornate.

BAUHAUS The Bauhaus was a German school of design founded in Weimar by the well-known architect Walter Gropius. The school taught that the function of a building—its purpose—should determine the building's form. Many Bauhaus teachers were famous architects and artists, and the school helped make modern architecture and design popular.

CARICATURE Caricatures are drawings or other depictions of people that are meant to poke fun—or sometimes criticize—their subjects. These drawings resemble real people, but their facial features are usually exaggerated in a funny way.

CENTRAL PERSPECTIVE Central perspective allows you to depict three-dimensional objects on a two-dimensional (or flat) surface, and to show the object's correct proportions.

DECONSTRUCTIVISM Deconstructivism is an architectural style from the end of the 20th century. This style includes walls that aren't straight, unusual materials and colors, and complicated interior spaces. In much Deconstructivist architecture, it seems as if a giant has taken a building apart and then put it back together at random.

FRESCO A fresco is a kind of wall painting. Artists make frescos by covering the wall in plaster and then quickly painting over the plaster—as fresco paint dries rapidly.

GOTHIC The Gothic period began around 1140 in France and is the time of the great cathedrals. Gothic buildings often have pointed arches and many little turrets and ornamentation. The Renaissance brought this period to an end.

MODERNISM In the early 20th century, architects began to design buildings with simple shapes, modern materials such as concrete, and no fancy decoration. This kind of architecture came to be known as modern, Modernist, or contemporary.

MOORISH ARCHITECTURE This is the architecture of the Arab people who lived in Spain during the Middle Ages—and who still live in northern Africa.

NAVE The nave is a part of the church where people sit or stand during the worship service.

NEOCLASSICISM With Neoclassicism (c. 1750–1850), architects used ideas and styles from ancient Greece and Rome. Classical buildings are usually stiffer and more formal than Baroque architecture.

PILGRIMAGE CHURCH In Catholic Christianity, churches built in out-of-the-way places often contain important relics (or artifacts) of saints and other holy people. People make "pilgrimages" (or long journeys) to visit these churches.

PLAGUE This is the architecture of the Arab people who lived in Spain during the Middle Ages.

PRE-FABRICATED In modern architecture, many parts of a building are made in advance at a factory. These parts are known as pre-fabricated (or pre-made).

RENAISSANCE The age of the Renaissance lasted from 1400 to the end of the 16th century. This term comes from a French word that means "born again". Renaissance architects and artists helped "rediscover" and re-use the styles of ancient Greece and Rome.

REPUBLICAN A republican form of government is one without kings or queens. Republican leaders are elected. The United States and many other countries have a republican form of government.

UNESCO WORLD HERITAGE SITE UNESCO is an organization of the United Nations, which is responsible for preserving human culture around the world. The World Heritage Site label is given to monuments and works of art that need protection because of their outstanding significance.

Answers to the Quiz Questions

Page 11:   Francesco Borromini helped Bernini build the Baldachin* above the grave of St. Peter.

Page 14:   Christopher Wren designed the first rain gauge sensor in 1661,
             which allows you to measure rainfall.

Page 16:   You can see Balthasar Neumann at the bottom of the fresco—sitting next to a big dog!

Page 20:   Benjamin Latrobe's best-known structure is the United States Capitol building in Washington, D.C..
             As the third President of the United States, Jefferson spent a lot of time in this building!

Page 44:   Zaha Hadid designed a revolving stage for the "Pet Shop Boys" for their Nightlife Tour in 1999.

© Prestel Verlag, Munich · London · New York, 2014

© for the works reproduced is held by the architects and artists, their heirs or assigns, with the exception of: Frank Lloyd Wright and Mies van der Rohe: VG Bild-Kunst, Bonn 2014; Le Corbusier: FLC / VG Bild-Kunst 2014; Zaha Hadid: Zaha Hadid 2014; Frank Gehry: Frank Gehry, LLP 2014

Front Cover:
Frank Gehry, Guggenheim Museum, Bilbao
Frank Lloyd Wright, Fallingwater, Pennsylvania
Filippo Brunelleschi, Cathedral Dome, Florence

Frontispiece: Frank Gehry, Walt Disney Concert Hall, Los Angeles

Picture Credits:
akg-images, Berlin: Cover top (Olimpia Torres), Cover middle (Universal Images Group / Universal History Archive), p. 4 (Manuel Cohen), 8 and 9 (Bildarchiv Monheim), 11 (Joseph Martin), 13 (Andrea Jemolo), 16 (Bildarchiv Monheim), 19 (Bildarchiv Monheim), 26 (Manuel Cohen), 28 (Universal Images Group / Universal History Archive), 31 (L. M. Peter), 35 (MPortfolio / Electa), 36 top, 36 below (Paul Almasy); Alexandra Cabri: p. 38 top; Carol M. Highsmith: p. 40, 41, frontispiece; Bernard Gagnon: p. 27; Frank Gehry, LLP: p. 38 below; Gettyimages: p. 12, p. 44; Brigitte Lacombe: p. 42 top; Laif: Cover below (Patrice Hauser); p. 6 (Zoratti, Ambience, Arcaid); p. 14 (Martin Sasse); LOOK-foto: p. 21, 23, 30–32 (age fotostock), 34 (Daniel Schoenen), 37 (Photononstop), 39 (age fotostock); Thomas Mayer: p. 43; Scala-Images: p. 17; The Bridgeman Art Library: p. 24, 25; Zaha Hadid: p. 42

Illustrations on pages 10 and 30: Annette Roeder
Illustrations in contents and timelines: Maria Krause

Prestel,
A member of Verlagsgruppe Random House GmbH
www.prestel.com

Prestel Publishing Ltd.   Prestel Publishing
14-17 Wells Street   900 Broadway, Suite 603
London W1T 3PD   New York, NY 10003

Library of Congress Control Number is available; British Library Cataloguing-in-Publication Data: a catalogue record for this book is available from the British Library; Deutsche Nationalbibliothek holds a record of this publication in the Deutsche Nationalbibliografie; detailed bibliographical data can be found under: http://dnb.ddb.de

Prestel books are available worldwide. Please contact your nearest bookseller or one of the above addresses for information concerning your local distributor.

Translation: Paul Kelly
Copyediting: Brad Finger
Layout: Meike Sellier, Eching
Conceptual Design: Michael Schmölzl, agenten.und.freunde, Munich
Production: Astrid Wedemeyer
Origination: ReproLine Mediateam, Munich
Printing and Binding: Printer Trento, Trento

Verlagsgruppe Random House FSC® N001967
The FSC®-certified paper Hello Fat Matt has been produced by mill Condat, Le Lardin Saint-Lazare, France.

ISBN 978-3-7913-7184-9